Circle the picture that belongs with the first one.

Circle the picture that belongs with the first one.

Circle the picture that belongs with the first one.

Circle the picture that belongs with the first one.

Circle the picture that belongs with the first one.

Circle the picture that belongs with the first one.

Circle 2 pictures that make a pair.

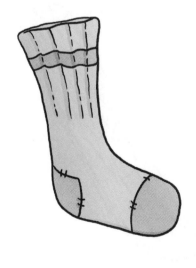 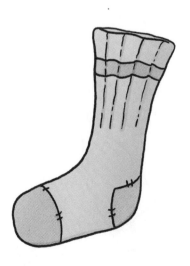 

Circle 2 pictures that make a pair.

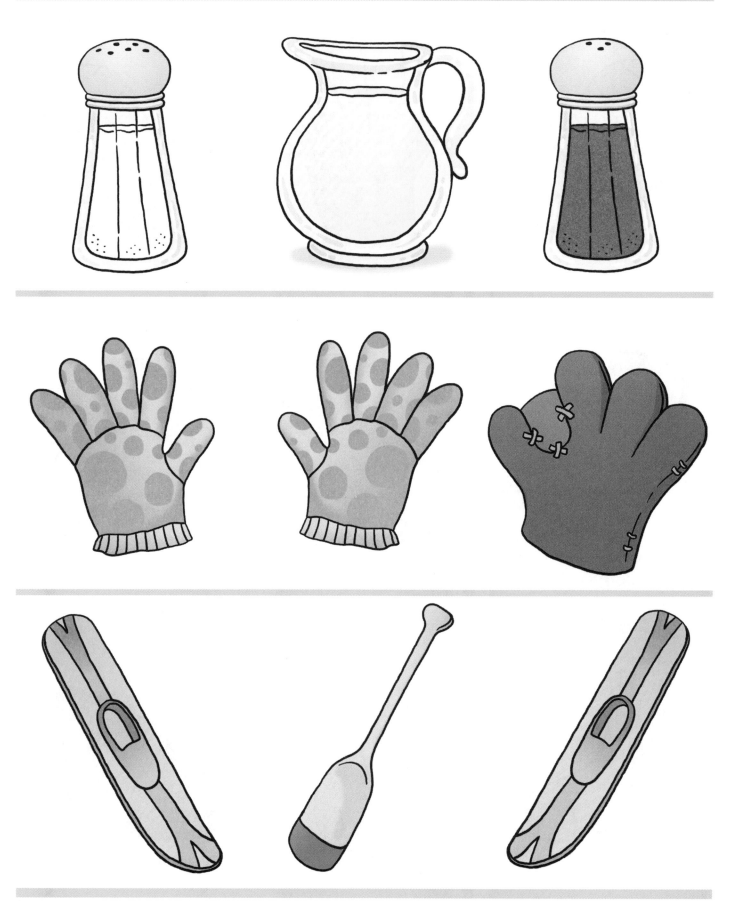

Circle 2 pictures that make a pair.

Circle **2** pictures that make a **pair**.

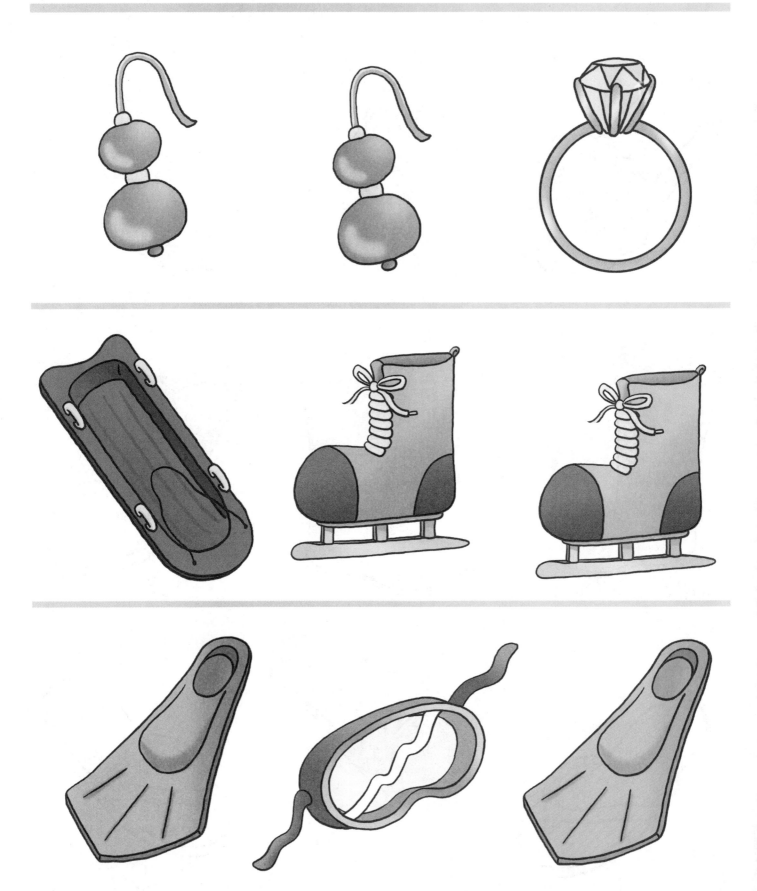

Circle **3** things that **belong** in the ice cream store.

Circle **3** things that **belong** in the school.

Circle 3 things that belong in the zoo.

Circle 3 things that belong at the beach.

Circle **2** pictures that **belong** with the big one.

Circle 2 pictures that belong with the big one.

Circle 2 pictures that belong with the big one.

Circle **2** pictures that **belong** with the big one.

Circle **2** pictures that **belong** with the big one.

Circle **2** pictures that **belong** with the big one.

Circle the picture that does **not belong** in each group.

Circle the picture that does **not belong** in each group.

Circle the picture that does **not belong** in each group.

Circle the picture that does **not belong** in each group.

Circle the picture that does not belong in each group.

Circle the picture that does **not belong** in each group.

Circle what does **not belong** in the picture.

Circle what does **not belong** in the picture.

Check Out

$0.00

Circle what does **not belong** in the picture.

Circle what does **not belong** in the picture.

Circle what does **not belong** in the picture.

31

Circle what does not belong in the picture.